Goldfish in a Baby Bath

The publishers gratefully acknowledge the support of

The Arts Council/An Chomhairle Ealaíon.

ÁINE MILLER

Goldfish in a Baby Bath

To Dear Catharine,
A little patch of blue+gold+sea.
A little piece of me in Barcelona.
Love You.
Brenda.
24 Dec 93

SALMON POETRY

First published in 1994 by
Salmon Publishing Limited,
A division of Poolbeg Enterprises Ltd,
123 Baldoyle Industrial Estate
Baldoyle, Dublin 13, Ireland.

© Aine Miller 1994

The moral right of the author has been asserted.

A catalogue record for this book is available from the British Library.

ISBN 1 897648 11 1

All rights reserved. No part of this publication may be reproduced or transmitted in any form or by any means, electronic or mechanical, including photography, recording, or any information storage or retrieval system, without permission in writing from the publisher. The book is sold subject to the condition that it shall not, by way of trade or otherwise, be lent, resold or otherwise circulated without the publisher's prior consent in any form of binding or cover other than that in which it is published and without a similar condition, including this condition, being imposed on the subsequent purchaser.

Front Cover Illustration by Treasa Flynn
Back Cover Photograph by James G Maguire
Cover design by Poolbeg Group Services Ltd
Set by Mac Book Limited in Palatino
Printed by The Guernsey Press Limited,
Vale, Guernsey, Channel Islands.

For Alex
Síle, Eilís, Angela, Michael
with love

Some of these poems have previously appeared
in the following publications:

*Acorn, Cloverdale Anthology of Irish Poetry 1992, Corpus,
Fatchance, First Time, Flaming Arrows, Fortnight, Fountain,
Interim, The Kerryman, Limerick Poetry Broadsheet, Orbis,
Odyssey, Pennine Platform, Poetry Ireland Review, Poets
Aloud Abu, The Rialto, Riverine, Sense of Place Broadsheet
(Poetry Ireland/Co-op. North), Six of Gold (The Works,
Wexford), Spectrum, The Steeple, Visions, The Waterford
Review, West Coast (Glasgow), Women's Work I & IV.*

Some were broadcast on The Arts Show, RTE, Radio
Kerry, Radio North-East.

Contents

Goldfish in a Baby Bath	1
Going Home	2
Da	4
Winter	5
The Silence Cloth	6
The Visit	8
Walls	9
Catherine's Clock	11
Girls	12
Mother Tongue	13
A Memory of School	14
Two Women Under the Lamp	15
Visitation	16
A Moment	18
Revolution	19
Caesura	21
A Blind Eye	23
Farsighted	24
Late Summer	25
Grandfather	27
Waking at Night	29
Mass at Inishgall	30
Dave	32
Evening	33
The Undertaker Calls	34
The Day Before Tomorrow	36

In the Garden at Barna	37
Seventeen	38
Marie	40
Photograph at Church Bay	41
Brown Stew with Dumplings	42
Meeting	43
Two Coffins	46
Apple Pie Order	47
Emigrant	48
The Lilies Have Had Their Day	49
Catherine	50
Emerson House	57
Lee Shore	59
Hung at the End of the Bed	63
Incorporation	64
Chair	65
Upright Freezer as a Wedding Gift	66
Pruned	67
You & son	68
The Day is Gone	69
Funny the Way	70
In the Word	72
Ding-Dong Bell	73
Ever Such	74
Pickpocket	76
Sojourner	77
Grey Area	78
Butter Balls	80

Heart Machine	81
In Djouce Woods	83
Woman Seated Under the Willows	85
Saturday Rugger Practice	86
Basement	88
Woman and Haystack	92
A Cliché Called Death	93
The Road to Navan	94
Non-Verbal Arts	95
At the Orchard Gallery – Derry	96
Miss Tynan to Willie Yeats	97

Goldfish in a Baby Bath

Sliver. Orange. Overspill of light.
All business,
cease that powering about,
streamtailing it
through the tangle of the everyday.

My image shades your element.

Rise to this pure colour,
the grace I sprinkle here, in flakes.

Going Home

Going home is uphill
all the way, steps unlearn
their level best, shuffle off
easy shoes grown comfy
on flat lands of the now.

Then is a steep incline –
even with a run at it –
leaning into Summerhill
the heart inside its rigging
knots. Lungs flap clammily.

A breather at St. Patrick's
down poxy steps with edges
smooth as soap, railings
nesting in the rust of
decades.   God is still

in view. Luminous above
communion cloth, and borne
upon the tongue again
past tuppences on baize,
confetti. Scent of freesias

makes you come gasping up
again, across York Hill and
Marie Celine, time contracting
as in painful spurts
you blunder headlong on

up, clutching at memory
(the way you held hands tightly
or linked an arm) only
to find no handholds now
clawing at empty air

till the gravel crunching
under your naked foot
you come on the implacable
black of that hall door,
brasses green with waiting.

Da

I could tell by the cut of him
he was well-oiled, feathering up the Hill

ahead of me; my mother'd have his
dinner on a pot, his hide for garters.

He couldn't care less, shambled once only
to a run, as with purpose, soon forgotten.

In black suit, shiny, a heat-dazed beetle,
he seemed smaller than I knew him. Sometime

at a standstill fumbling all his pockets
stared at empty hands, puffy, inept. Again

walked cocky, hitching trousers, squared-up
at passers-by. Fighting fit. I saw

heads turn, a small boy miming in his wake.
Below his coat, the white tail of his shirt

caught and held me. In a gauze of shame
I dawdled in a doorway, Hanley's windowing

his recession beyond the line of duty.
No cock crowed twice, I told myself that

my denial only mirrored his, a fact
that gave a little comfort then. Not now.

Winter

At Christmas only,
she'd take a glass,
'the first this year.'

He made a ceremony
of it, sherry
'brown as your hair.'

Warm tones
in spots of
colour on her cheeks.

Thumb and forefinger
on the stem, little
finger out, spilling.

Droplets, we were
shy of her loud
laugh, bold eye.

His hand on her.

The Silence Cloth

Mother brought it from *The North*,
an inward land way off the point

in Cork, a land of *once* and *used to be*
grown to the stuff of silence. This cloth

red dark chenille and bobble-fringed,
rough-textured as the cat's tongue,

clogged the sideboard drawer
so fully, the lock teeth didn't meet,

opened spontaneously. We fancied sighs
from that winy mouth, heard nothing

but the faint knocking of worms
in the wood, the shimmy of prisms.

When we were left to mind the house
we unleashed the cloth, hung it

as a curtain in the archway.
Hamlet's speeches ballooned our sails.

We rode on rhetoric. With bare bodkins
silenced the pratings of old men.

Spread across the dully shining heart
of the French mahogany table

at Christmas, it served its true purpose.
Under the skin of damask and Irish lace

it lay like an unhealed bruise,
while we pretended to be ordinary,

swopped Christmas cracker jokes,
affecting not to see how cut glass

indented silence, and the little stabs
of fork tongues left holes slow to heal.

The Visit
after a painting by Edouard Vuillard

In that red frock – shapeless
as a gymslip – collared in
pure white, held dead centre

by the light, my hands are clumsy
on the tray, china cups tilt
awkwardly. Drops spill from

the silver pot shiny for your
coming. Off the Dublin train.
A taxi to our door. Powdery cheek.

Pearls at your throat. Pale
leather on your tiny feet. 'How ...
long ... you are!' you say, veiled

eyes mocking. Mother's hand hides
a smile. Murmuring politely
I retire slyly into the picture

behind my eyes. Another girl
leans straining breasts across
a sill. Some crooning love song

holds her from this room
full of colluding women, eyes
speculative, mannikins in boxes.

Walls

On the right side
of our party wall they kicked
with the other foot, slept
late on Sundays, hung out
no bunting at Corpus Christi, kept

the gate to their garden locked,
our tree allowed us plunder
Eden with our stares, perfect
lawn the pond the duck, rose
arbour and summerhouse, a wonder

we even tried to copy, walled
little beds, sowed dahlias
red poppies Love-in-a-mist, then
tiring, kicked at failures,
let things seed, that wild time

loudhailed from sleep, we tumbled
out, the stair-wall bulged
like proving dough, gave heat, as
down our bare feet stumbled
out onto the terrace. Next Door

belched darkness, from the chimney
sparks flew, our neighbours smaller
in their nightclothes, failing
to salvage curtains, hauled
carpets in a nest of hoses, hissing

our stair wall cooled, leaked a little
pity, from her store
my mother gave her all
next door, cake, comfort,
only walls divided us, then

I was sick, they brought beef tea
and roses, before the fall
nasturtiums fired the summerhouse,
reached orange arms across the wall
to link with our convolvulus.

Catherine's Clock

To mark time
Done
They gave her a clock

Slime-green squatter
On the mantel
Between The Graces
Kept time

A sleepless prisoner,
Belying
Winged hours
With brass-rimmed seal

Cased
Her working life
In marble
I opened
When she died

Let time fly.
It circles only
Lacks the wherewithal
To follow her

Beyond the rim
Her eternal dance
Unmeasured
By its blinking
Eye.

Girls

Orphans, up from the country,
They walked the pram, did the fires,
Slept in the back kitchen.

We called them all Chrissie.

On Patrick's Bridge
The street photographer captured us
Two in the pram, and Chrissie.
I, in pleated bonnet, velour coat,
Downturning mouth, always my back to
My hooded sister. Eyes for Chrissie

Only, the Lee wind swirled
Chrissie's hair across
Her face, crazed eyebrow, underlip.
A puzzle. Piecemeal.

  – Playing at peep her sharp nose
  around the kitchen door pus-
  covered thumb cut on serrated
  edged tin of peas zippered flesh
  above black stockings when she pegged
  washing out to dry a wall eye
  downy lip alpaca lap smell of
  caustic Lifebuoy soap mintoes
  kissy mouths Holy Gods giggles –

The crinkled picture holds her
Still, a series by herself, Chrissie.

Mother Tongue

'Shibbies' – her word for us
Hanging behind, with no chit-chat,
Tongues thick as wash leathers.

Thick and 'sonsy' her other words,
Like College scarves marking us off
As blow-ins, she was proud of that.

Northern burr, a 'lilty' perching
On a Hill in Cork, she kept her feet dry,
salted language to keep it ours.

Though native as our first cries
At the Marie Celine made us,
Sing-song thickened into silence.

We waited the catalyst of exile
To let the mother tongue
Sweet-talk through parched mouths.

A Memory of School

The window frames a black sky,
my tired brain struggles
with the algebra of stars,

wars with equations
that threaten the mystery.

Sister Ena turns from the board,
her pointer prods too,

'You noodle you,' she singsongs
in the broad Cork, 'You

noodle you,' she hisses
from a goose's coif.

Recoiling in umbrage
I look it up in the dictionary,

'A witless fellow,' it still says.
And should.

A loon, a gligeen who puzzles
signs in a night sky still,
wills one unanswerable question.

Two Women Under the Lamp
after a painting by Edouard Vuillard

Nights under the lamp, us children lit
to our beds, his chair overstuffs the room
like huffy silence –

                     Not even chintz, a blaze
of daytime bloom, she corded, pleated, skirted
on the swelling frame, diminishes it.

Growing, as the shadows grow, it elongates
from chair to throne to marriage bed,
becomes unmentionable –

                     Whatever it is she's at
is now a blur, shaping doilies or a collar,
she's in the ha'penny place.

Her sister gathering all, the red
of passion at her back, one up on
unwise virgins –

                 waits placidly
his key in lock, the iron bar dropped
home. The summons. And the coming.

The other reddens, draws closer to the lamp,
with scarf of light around her shoulders
solicits day.

Visitation

I must be very sick, he's come up so far,
I thought, when he shone around the door,
and stood beaming by my bed, an alien
on linoleum acre.

The shutters were across, perhaps I'd measles,
a fire in the grate, and Catherine
brought me grapes I couldn't eat, Mi-Wadi,
on the mantelpiece.

A yellow candle under grey Blessed Oliver,
whose cavalier locks I coveted till
they told me how, poor Noll, at Drogheda
he lost them.

At the nape my hair sticky, eyeballs
raw in hot sockets, each muscle-clenching
swallow bypassed a cannonball in
my furred throat.

Tell you what, he said, when I turned from
warm milk, we'll make a cocktail, a dash
of lemon cordial 'll do the trick, 'twill
sweeten it.

Even I knew better than that, laughed
as it curdled, again as my astonishing,
my displaced father spilt thickened milk
on the nursery floor.

There now, he said, you're on the mend,
winked at Blessed Oliver, his pursed mouth,
we'll tell them down below 'twas that grey man
who soured it.

His whiskey sour kiss was sweet as new milk
on my skin, his thumb in leather sling
plucked rabbits from the shadows
on grey walls.

He hummed the song at twilight, Love's Old
Sweet, the proof he'd been was
spilt milk scabbed on linoleum, asking for
a good scald.

A Moment

Now
On Clarke's Bridge
I hear the river stop.
The weir waits in vain.

Your high bike
Deadlocks.

Your skirt a fan –
A pigeon's wing
For take-off – brushing my knees.

Tears stay on the cheek
I bury in your cape,
My small hands around you are
Numb.

In my schoolbag
Milk stops dripping. The white
Pencil case you bought me –
Its lead's sharp, new rubber –

Revolution
Hungary, October 1956

This was the only storm
we did not talk up
over teacups and saucer-
shaped buns in the Rest,

where Aquinas was used to
being flashed in the pan-
cake pale face of
existentialists, me

who thought love was the only
bolt from the blue
and Saints did their Marching
to Mick Delahunty's drums,

till thunder of tanks rolling
through Hungary, the young,
become men in the strain of one
night, took to Cork streets

in phalanx, high talk bitten down
to quickening thrum of
blood, followed a half-masted flag
in slow march; one drunk,

stepping to drums much older,
kicked in the window
of the Queen's Old Castle,
shame crackled above us,

lightning Red Cross refusal
to take volunteers
lit up my sky, 'Too bad,'
I lied like the troopers.

Caesura

An adverbial clause,
the when
of her going
hangs on my days.

I pause
between visits,
to find grammar in our love,
a compound of prepositions, the list

she made me rhyme
when I came to her for a start
in my Composition, or
to have spellings heard,

trips off my tongue easily
as the years:
about above according to, across after against,
along amid amidst among amongst around,
at before behind below beneath between
betwixt, by concerning during excepting for
from into ...

at into falters ... still
no mistress of what comes after,
to govern relationship,
define an absence.

I want nothing
other than the common
noun she makes proper, Mother,
and wordless pause before I stumble on

without

A Blind Eye

There were signs
had she a weather eye
cocked, sense to comb
folk memory for lore,
patterns in the lie

of land, to note depressions
deepening, nuances
in wind direction, rash
berry-reddening
in prickly silences.

Evidence enough
when fulmination of clouds
shadowed pale days, suspicious
sudden flush, the proof as snow-
fall, full, allows

her this obliteration,
swifly absolute,
of such markings on the sand
as the Follow Me
imprints of an Athenian prostitute.

In a wilderness, she waits,
eyes still raw,
watches cocksure birds track wastes,
their weather eyes
bright for signs of thaw.

Farsighted

Lonely in the Dublin Hills,
Sweeping distance: 'On a clear day
One can see the Mournes.'

I see only you, Mother,
That hospital bed in Cork,
March cold and cut flowers.

In a clouded pane you show me
Yourself, a bigboned girl
On a high bike, freewheeling.

The road to Carlingford,
A works' outing, seeing miles of
Strand at Cooley – and the Mournes

On a clear day.

Late Summer

Clematis
that stormed walls in May,
opts for the horizontal.

Its tendrils,
lackadaisical,
in middle-age fall short,

shade the snail's
random silvery trails,
mysteries on the patio,

where I lie
in wait, milky white
furniture in readiness.

Parasol,
shadow men in whites,
and diamonds big as the Ritz

in patterns
on the table-top.
Its veneer close-to is cracked,

curled upon
itself revealing
liver spots, dead insects, ants.

Crestfallen
pigeons seek in vain
where hopes are worn to shadow.

And blood dries
from red ants that climb
to death instanter on this

notebook slab.
All things in check, ghosts
laid of possibility.

And in cracks
a cankerous weed
maintains deadly stitchery.

Grandfather

Alive for me only in stories,
he was a giant,

a big noise in the Vincent de Paul,
photographs prove
he looked like God the Father
and Parnell, a wonder then

he took the nod from up above
in deciding between
those with little and with less

– when chickens hopped onto a hot griddle
pecked at popping oatmeal in the pot
he knew that for a Sign, left discreetly
parcels on the whitened step –

a graven image
in his daughter's eye, she passed on
how he, a pilgrim with her to St. Winifred
in Wales, took on the Devil singlehanded,
floored that soft-soaping sassenach
with doctrine, she swore he vanished
from their carriage, left a poker burn
to prove he'd been,

in my head he then became a cross
between
St. Patrick and Fr. Willie Doyle,

for all his size
she kept him tidy
in the box under her bed

the one she never let us see the inside of

when she closed her eyes
that last time, then I dared
look for him, found my grandfather

held him in the cupping of my hands,
a poem, gold-rimmed spectacles, a pipe,
a clutch of yellowed diaries bled him
to the minutiae of his dying,

stripped of his image in her eye
what my grandfather *is*
is elsewhere

Waking at Night

There was a picture on that wall –
Aunt Catherine's pansies in a pot,
the frame worth looking at –
surely? It's there inside my head,

as is the locker, lamp, bedside rug
behind that fall of inky doubt.
No need to stretch even a foot,
I trust they're there. Beyond this bed

all is as was. Why then this blinding
sense of loss and dislocation,
slippage of faith in the unseen,
this night-bound void? The red-

eyed clock-radio blinks four zeros. Sum
or the subtraction? A touch will tell.
Night Music, shipping forecast, spell
out my position. Fog. In the dead

uncertainty of night, what is exact
between the idea and the fact?

Mass at Inishgall
The Island of the Stranger
– to Edna O'Brien

The priest
opens his arms
to embrace the strangers
kneeling where rain makes grasses hang
their heads.

A child
sings a solo
lifting up hearts and eyes
to where memory is circling
whitely.

They've cut
all the nettles
down for this day only
she remembers their stinging white
blisters.

Ringing
the altar round,
touching his garment hem,
juices weeping from bruised stems, are
dock leaves.

Waves splash
and recede, splash
and recede, ask, receive,
ask, receive, asking, receiving,
asking.

Dave

Every morning he stripped his bed,
folded bedding into a pile, each day
a gamble, his return at evening
a long shot always. This the first lesson

learnt in two world wars. Luck of the draw,
victory over that hill, or the next, only
if you play your cards right, the certainty,
a stockstill soldier is a dead one. So

life was kitbagged, ready for the off,
in photo frames, his daughter, four forever,
ballet-dances Buttercup in the school play,
his wife, a collie at her heels, shades eyes

against a setting sun, two boys
bat cricket balls on a childhood green,
an everlasting innings. This way,
light to carry, they left room enough

for Littlewoods, St. Bruno tin, pink racing paper
daydreams of the treble, St. Leger, Derby,
Gold Cup on his birthday, a pound said
Gunners for the Double. Sure things.

When he came to visit, left with us
the suitcase full of photographs, we knew
the odds had grown too heavy,
the Finish was a matter of time.

Evening

Starling sheets across the sky
fall like monofilament on trees,
while puffed-up weeds release
soft loads to winds of chance – maybe

it's not too late to catch
remaining light, though every wing,
like every year, brushes with it
cobwebs of the dark, a mesh

that once made treetops burn
with incandescent sunshine. Still
I make a composite of what stays
in the half-dark, hold my breath

for white owls nesting in the barn
the gleam of that first star.

The Undertaker Calls

In black kid
shoes, dark-suited, trim
as a shipping clerk, the case on knees,

it was all despatch, the forms in line,
'Your mother's name? Date of birth?'
the leaving of it all

to him, 'I'll ring The Times ...
get the Night Desk yet,' in my extremity
I half-expected

unction, but no such thing, he
was true
as honey, his voice

mellifluous, candour
in his eye, 'You have a plot?
No trouble there,'

or anywhere, sign here,
again here, rest in me,
he touched his lips

with whiskey, left
that special crystal
on the floor,

nothing to worry, his chamois feet
have picked their way
through pyramids

of lilies, sidestepped
limestone chips,
never been caught

wrongfooted
at the lip of a dark hole,
learned to walk

so lightly on water
skin, the surface
of my grief

may still delay
a decent interval to break
and spill.

The Day Before Tomorrow

What am I thinking as I sit at that window
alone, my notes before me, the future huge
as an exam? The trains are there. On the go.

Oncoming. The river underlines the sky.
INNISFALLEN's flying colours any minute now
pass by, England bound. My last summer.

Pre-occupying the room behind, childhood is
asleep in the iron bed. The brown suitcase
has been dusted off, waits. From a height

I see the party in the Rector's garden. Games
on a lawn. Time for tea. The birthday girl
throws a cut branch. Longtressed laburnum

catches in the yew. Today is in suspense.
She stays to watch it shimmer. And I too.
It playacts living. A portent. Or a promise.

In the Garden at Barna

The present is pushy, full of itself.

Marigolds bat their lashes at me,
grasses are frantically waving.
The bog deal elbows the hydrangea,
griselinias call attention to themselves
by constant fidget.
Anything to catch my eye.

> Beyond, the sea, sudsy, busy,
> gathers and launders the sky's greys,
> carrying on. Gulls
> dazzle to a white horizon.

Across the Bay, Clare, harbours the inward.
The mind's rays light it in
and out of focus. Memories
gloom behind a shower.
The break when it comes is radiance.

> Now sees some shift,
> that hedge, those firs, wall, my bulk,
> budge up.

The past is on the move again.

Seventeen

I had on a terrible frock,
red check that rustled, my hair in a bang,
a brooch shaped like a poodle dog,

even so at that social you sang
Granada in my ear only, taught me
to the tune of *Jealousy* the tango,

though when we walked across the City,
the two of us in my swagger coat,
arms twined, we lumbered clumsily

as three-legged runners, quoting
Spanish poems as our touching pulses beat
Latin rhythms, the secrets told

more for lovers than for such as me
and you, yet every bit as binding, more,
they're still unspoken, but when we

kissed across the bicycle at my door,
shy as seedlings forced into the light,
we butted noses like a pair of Eskimos,

you muttered gruff goodbyes, took flight
down Summerhill, with borrowed bike and clips,
for one whole minute in the light

of dining-room mirror, my lips
grazed by the hair of your unshaven chin,
were wide awake, beautiful.

Marie

I had forgotten you till now

when October trees are firing the clay of sky

at eighteen you were already an autumn landscape

in the Ladies' Club at college you stripped off
slung the cream sweater on a stool, stood bare
only in the Fifties such behaviour was extreme
we were uncomfortable with it, looked away

while you poured the fire of your hair into a basin

in that burnt sienna skirt, bare feet, you were all
hurting orange and smoke

a fire that blazed too early

when you touched my arm years later at a Conferring
I looked for Marie
found ashes
pale hair pinned behind your ears
a grey pinstripe suit.

Photograph at Church Bay

        That was the girl
      in a dirndl
    opening knees
  unladylike
as the tide came
  licking winy
    up the cobs and bread
      roll boulders of
        that shore
       on the edge of then
          Turning
      her head up
     to catch at
    every ounce of
   the future that was
spraying salty rumours
    and a blessing
      light as chrism
       on her lips
        as they felt its kiss
          Promises
       kept
     with a vengeance
     battered her into
    the present
where the woman is
     back to the rock
       in this congregation of stones
        Standing
       her ground
       for dear life.

Brown Stew with Dumplings

*– The October clay of sky,
   oncoming rain, migraine –*

She sieved white flour
Watching it float and fall.

Saw this evanescence
Thicken into balls,
Pastecoloured,
On a kitchen plate, a summary.

*– Whey face in kitchen glass,
   buttoned-up, coarsegrained –*

She put a lid on them, trusting
The air she captured
In that first free fall,
A little warmth.

Meeting
after the painting 'The Blue Girl'
by Mainie Jellett

I

Sketching
her with my eyes
shut.

Knowing that look,
head on one side,
smile.

For that horny devil
broken out
into the aftergrass.

In fields
beyond her head
he gambols.

Till she collars him,
settles him down,
with a third Hail Mary,

on the flip side
of her haloing
hair.

II

Only one foot
strayed
from the bed
of her girlhood.

She cradles
its match
on the edge
of the simple.

Quilt
stained by the shadow
of the girl
who poses.

In a room
full of moonlight
a question mark
childish.

III

Outside the moon's reach
the woman waits,
her glow the residue
of tides.

She knows the moment
of footfall, then
the unaltering trudge
of years.

Her pencil lingers.
The past is still
black and white as a dream.
There's time.

For the girl will turn,
their eyes will meet,
flood with recognition
of kin.

Suffusing the sketch
with gold and blue,
the mapmaker's colours
of old.

Discover the girl,
in a blue dress,
hesitant at the edge
of me.

Two Coffins

Her coffin stands in centre aisle
       while I, and her mourners,
            file closely to receive
Communion.
       She was someone's mother,
                   daughters
fill a pew.
   Someone's wife, sister,
          neighbours group
for a purple wreath.
       Sheaves of mass cards
            warm the pale wood
when I reach out my hand
       to touch her.
            As I pass,
another coffin
       slipped into the Dublin docks,
            is hastily despatched
by road North.
       Who will lay hands
            on this one
the baggage handlers
       at Aldergrove
            would not touch?

Apple Pie Order

You have to be an Anglo-Saxon to peel them so
Methodically, your circling steel strips green
In one bandage, bares white underflesh.
With two sharp chops quarters part
Like provinces. Those divided remnants
Pincered between thumb and first finger are
Gouged, flesh sliced to crescent lookalikes
Laid out in rows for identification, rigid
In the cold case, dusted with sugar, lemon juice
The expected tart, under crimped lips.

Sharp contrast the memory of my own mother
Turning each green globe in her random hand,
Parings fall like petals, light
Irregular wafers of the flesh, layered like memories
Brown-sugared, the crust on its inverted cup
Flakes in the oven, hot kitchen smells, sweetness
Spiced with clove, her truly Celtic excess
A core well worth the waiting.

Emigrant

It cost him, I knew,
twelve pounds ten shillings,
a fortune then, it was understood

I had to go,
rail against or no, and every evening
for my fare he grimly
from his pockets drew handfuls
of brass threepences,
'Save those in the jar,' he said,

and as their level rose he too
became a whole heap more accustomed, so

when I heard him say, 'Not a brass farthing
do I care, go or stay, love's not worth tuppence
anyway,' I knew it wasn't true,
or even nearly,
the precious unguent of his quayside tear, was balm
more dear than spikenard
from a broken jar.

The Lilies Have Had Their Day

Last blossoms
pennons
on forked stems.

Arsenal of catapults
two fingering
the sky.

Withdrawal of sun
in a huff of cloud.
Shadows

free to stretch
wings
across the garden.

Dark
in their wake
a flooding stain.

Drowning in gloom
a supplication
of lilies.

Catherine
Sketches for a Portrait

I

She crocheted stars in cotton thread
Moulded polyanthus heads from wax
Stencilled roses on satin cushions
Appliqued orchids on to union cloth
Embroidered Jacobean leaves on screens
Stitched pomegranates in lemon silks
Drew threads to hem the finest lawn
Painted flamingos at the School of Art
Fingered music from piano strings

Flowered on a single stem.

II

Summer Sundays she sat upright on a rock,
ankles neatly crossed, never the knees,
a long-sleeved dress, two strings of pearls.

Always a hat, no lecherous sun to leach
the careful amber of her hair
or reach behind dark glasses, paper fan,
to penetrate Fair Natural powder layer,
kiss her maiden skin.

Three-dimensional too scant a form
for her objective presence on the beach,
she was theatre in the round, the player
and the play, for us to circle, slow
unroll of nylons her performance art.

Discreet as Sunday the lifting of that hem,
she palmed the home-made garters, popped pink
suspenders under arty silk of knicker legs,
pale plump flesh peeled of service weight,
she dallied in the shallows, let the sea
at her corns.

III

She raised her voice
only in sleep,
hoarse gutturals fracturing the fine bone
of my night time casing, so
startled me from slumber I lay awake
in a fall of darkness,
crossed small arms
against the Devil-man she wrestled.

Slept again
only when the shouting lulled
to the grumble of her snore,
even strokes
restoring wholeness
in my sky resetting her
as constant star.

IV

Sometimes
on my way from school
I called to see her at the Office.

She sounded different
talked in elocution.

I stood outside the counter at Dispatch
hoped to see Mullany,
or my Uncle Dan (if I were lucky
he'd give me a Sweet Afton tin
for pencils, or a cigar box
to decorate with lace or shells).

She looked smaller,
a face and shoulders at the hatch
like the ticket lady at the Palace.
Uncle Dan looked huge, all ginger tweed,
bristle, called her Miss McKey.

She gave me sixpence to go home.

V

She said Dromara
the way another woman talked of
Tara, word loamed with genealogies,

pointed at the painting on the wall,
'By your cousin Jimmy, from a photograph
this small,' she said, an impression of

well-tilled fields, touch of indigo in hedges,
blue of imprecision on the bases of the trees
screening the house – that hardly house,

more a fleck of flake white, glitter
in a dreaming eye – we humoured her
this history on the wall, well-framed,

the very best of gilt, 'Yours too,'
she always said, but for us children
true geography was more an issue.

'I'll go home, someday Sunday,'
elbow deep in suds she mouthed, 'Dromara,'
solace in its vague topography.

VI

Pirandello
might have written her in,
assigned her a definite, if minor, role
instead of which
like a bit player paid by the minute,
she made her entrances and exits
on cue, more
or less, pressed onstage.

Out into the action
to furiously ad lib
the Mother, Nanny, Upstairs Maid,
Aunt, (the Femme Fatale inside her head
outside her range).
Enough to cause a schizophrenia
in someone less convinced
her Author had the greatest faith
in her ability to pull her weight.

Besides
he was always in the wings
or prompter's box, to whisper stage directions,
set her straight, help her to create
the spurious reality, shadowy
prelude
in pursuit of which she earned
her starring role

elsewhere

VII

The bed was an island in an archipelago

her slippers beached currachs

'She's quiet now, but oh ...'
Sister's raised brows made waves enough.

*Still voyaging then, lightless,
over these new seas,
in your nightdress, a manic quest
for handbag, mascara, eyebrow tweezers
captured by pirates, lashes these
with filthy words
you'd wash our tongues for.*

*Who steers you now to safe harbour
turns love's deaf ear, blind eye?*

'I've it safe beside me,' she whispered,
handbag stowed like tottie under cover.

They propped her with a pillow, fluffed
amber hair, tied the sateen bow
under her chin, for visitors

took away the bars.

Her eyes saw past me, smile a radiance,
she clapped hands,
'What did I say! Here's De Valera now.'

A puzzled porter thought it was his birthday.

VIII

Afterwards the piano went too,
sweet as a kernel, true as its big-boned frame,
it was all hers, coming with her as it had
to take up residence in the space between
the carpet and the wall.

Heavy feet slippered,
the broad shoulder was no man's
land where we became her portion, nudging
relics of her own home, rose-coloured
vase with prisms, the biscuit barrel
my grandfather won in a walking race.

Here were our needed rainbows, inlaid
in mild mother of pearl, the wrapover warmth
of sheet music, a heart already overstrung,
we sheltered in their arc of sentiment
and melody, candlelit, illusory.

Yet nothing illusive about the upright,
black and white in parallel, never counter,
always in touch, in reach, in tune.

It took four strong men to shift it,
holland wrapped, hefted on their shoulders,
its lid rattled as they angled in the hall,
empty candlesconces knuckle-cracking, back
in the drawing room a bright rectangle, wall
paper fresh, the gilding virginal, intact.

Emerson House

A sideways look, enough,
halved the shock of its defacement,
the indignity of madonna blue
on window frames,
a primrose door, I turned from it.

Stared instead, through railings,
at a purple tree. Sprung from the hard
earth of the back terrace
where the bins had stood,
it quivered towards a crazy take-off,
some latter-day ascension, frantic
with the wings of tortoiseshells.

I clamped on railings,
marked my palms again with weeping stigmas
as I swung at arms' length
to and fro, a giddy arc
between the tree and house,
my skirts a winged sweep of memory.

If I should push on that hall door,
climb those stairs, forty years of stairs,
I'd meet on the top landing,
or in the window recess,
a girl in ankle socks,
the same green eyes as mine.

She chews her nail the way I do, is slow
to speak to any but herself.
But can I face
the dawn of recognition in her eye,
and its refusal,
before I manage to explain
how many years it takes to grow a tree,
how many more for it to be alive
with butterflies.

Lee Shore

The wind from across the river
raised the roof, slates made shift,
wearied, hung over.

Mornings after, slaters came to pin and tar,
tied their ladders to the area rails
with nylons, strangled blasphemies
as slates fell like guillotines
in the front yard, swore.

Swore they'd see the whole lot
to Kingdom Come, we sent them up
tea in the aluminium pot, sweet
milk in a pail, steadied their nerves,
they tossed us pennies –

> This Jill lived up The Hill
> afraid of water,
> not the Lee, bilious under the Bridge
> or foaming yellowly by St. Marie's of the Isle
> but buried river that tentacles below stone
> veins the City's underside, waits
> for time and tide and rains
> to flood the floors of Oliver Plunkett Street
> as underground subversion the lives
> at street level. I tiptoed on this floe
> of floating city, afraid to put a foot wrong,
> took the Eight bus to a safe height.

– the gas man counted on the deal,
scrubbed white, a jackpot
of coppers and bobs became a tower city,
his dirty fingers whooshed coins
into chimney stacks, the windfall
bought us sausages for tea, fed the hungry-
toothed meter mouth, saved the day –

> When brown ooze swashed toes
> and sandals slapped in treacheries of mud
> in The Glen, my cousins harnessed
> to the charge of me, eased that yoke
> telling of youngwans vanished
> in the swallows of the bog, teased me
> from stone to stone with promises,
> glassy streams to paddle, thorneens
> in a jam jar, early sightings of the Bad Boys.
> I shut my eyes and hitched
> to the tails of their cotton skirts
> leapt into the comfort of kinship, hollows
> deep as bogholes, bottomless as memory.

– the trapdoor to the terrace opened
for the coalman, he lurched each load over
his sacking-cornered head, white eyes
gave no sign he knew
what litters of wild cats he buried
with his slack landslide, enough
that we should sign the warrant,
the wisp of paper blackened by his thumb.

He proffered from behind his ear
a pencil stump, washed his hands of them,
unspoken for, their loss still rears –

> Still feel an undertow, my childhood
> lapped inside great arms, like Cork City,
> deltas etched on footsoles, now
> sweet-talk my way above mouthwaters
> in childish odyssey, home
> by Woolworth's, Cudmore's, The Cova,
> Miss Hanley's, Henchy's at the Cross,
> for bullseyes, satin pillows, cloverock,
> Jockeybars, allsorts, conversation lozenges,
> I sing-song litanies, keep afloat,
> a marshmallow on hot chocolate.

– at our kitchen sink Batt Gleeson
stirred his pails, touched the new distemper
with a Reckitt's blue, marked
each Spring, came every year
to whiten over ceiling stains, cream
and toffee brown like photo prints
where shifting slates had let the rain
and all the seepages of time and loss,
sheltering close, I watched his brush
banish ghosties, only dreamers see
the faces in old rooms now –

> in dream
> all is fluent,
> now and whenever run,

        marsh, house, inner city become
        awash

– in its floodtide living and dead may synchro-swim.
Filled to the gills with is and was and may be
I wallow in this ambivalence.

Hung at the End of the Bed

There
for the taking – a stockingful –
hopes, miracles, glimmering
in membrane, at full stretch,
childhood in knots.

The pod bulges, grown out of
recognition – a sugar mouse, pencil tin.

Global orange in the toe,
suspended at the nether end of optimism,
shrinks to wizened skin, papery scales.
Zestlessness.

Incorporation

Set against my need
   – I have to be alone
     inside my head –
Daughter, at the piano, picks out
Her tune, note by note, rearing,

The theme from The Black Stallion
Kicks down the stable door,
Bolts across my fields,
Hoofbeats drown out birdsong,
Harmonies of bees.

Astride, I go with him,
Move as one,
Uncircumscribed by hair or bone,
Slow to collected canter, walk.

The fields refilled with music,
When I slip from him
My new song rides
On iron hooves.

Chair

    This pine chair's real enough,
Has whatever substance it takes
To be finite. With me it makes
A four-square image in relief –
    Though shrunken in aged air,
Our round pegs sit too easily
In round holes, shift obligingly
In constant give and take of wear –
    Wearing our history well
Our ringed eyes mellowing can glaze
The memory of our greening days
Before the widowing axe fell –
    I am the parasite
Around its legs hooking my toes,
if move a muscle snagging hose,
I borrow bulk, afraid in light
    Alone I'm shadowless.

Upright Freezer as a Wedding Gift

We could nearly haw them
with our breath, the frosty
layers that first formed,
the decorative icing,
a touch of sparkle, hoar
we might thaw at blood heat –

we grew careless, let ice
thicken like cholesterol,
made shift in the narrowed
cavities, then a blitz
on the ice wall, soaking
up floods with bath towels –

honeymooning again,
such white space to play with
we could almost forget
ice forms from inside out,
groaning on convergence
pushes the door ajar.

Pruned

A minute of your time.

Slipped across the room – a surprise
Present – green room green walls
Green curtained tree. And rising

Up the years some old music
Max Bruch,
Kenneth McKellar's red red rose.

Sliding between the ribbons
Undid me – almost.

In the loosening,
I pressed my thumb deliberately
on the concealed thorn. Proud.

Proud I know subversion when I see it.

The past between your teeth, we cut
Again to brown,
Nipped below the node.

You & son

He pitches guesses,

an hundred million zillion
picked like stones for skimming
deeps of accuracy, the rapturous
clusters in his small head
pop like corn in a hot skillet.

'Don't exaggerate,' you say, 'Stop
being ridiculous,' at the same time
you insist you're having a Bite to eat,
Drop of tea, a Spot of bother.

'There's billions, Dad' – bees
in the lavender – evening
grumbles with their hum.
'Humbug,' you say, 'At most there's two
or three,' capture both in a jar

to prove it
a sad old year for bees, worse for boys
without the reassurance
of more infinitude in the possible
than occupies any jar, or ever bursts
the confines of a father's footprint.

The Day is Gone
for Angela

The day is gone
I pushed a buggy across the green,
claimed, as wagons did, new territories,
treadling fear into squares, familiar
as the Afghan rug
with which I wrapped you round
and had to have against your cheek
before you'd sleep.

I saw with your eyes
grass kneel at either side of us,
McGroarty's wolfish alo shrink to bow-wow,
the wino on a bench become
the Da-da from your picture book.

The future was no farther off
than where you'd kick your shoe,
its rebuckling my everpresent. Now

when I have to cross that green,
I hook my thumb in my handbag strap,
walk quickly
as if I had a purpose.

Funny the Way

Funny the way
he made us porridge,
soup plates of it,
when we came late
by trolley bus, from Holloway

Odeon, or a show
at the Hippodrome, Golders Green,
noses red, even my nipples sore
from extremes of cold
unknown in Cork,

temperate centre
of our earth's turning.
He served up theirs with sugar,
demerara from Tate & Lyle
pearled the surface

skin, foreign as the West Indian's
clipping tickets at Paddington,
or picking over sweet potatoes, yams,
at his pitch
on the Seven Sisters,

while I put salt on mine,
though sheeted Cellophane
held off the damp, and golden
curtains from the Co-op dreamed
sunshine, he regaled with

tales of Max Miller or Tessie O'Shea,
and funny the way he'd court a girl –
a show, chocolates, the bus home –
still have change from five bob,
until time for me to leave

him to take out his teeth,
fill the stone jar,
set the clock for five,
dream of horses
or the pools,

and I,
who found little to smile at then,
now never mention him
without beginning

funny the way ...

In the Word

Putting a name on things is how
I make some sense of what I see or feel –
the ache of all that greenery given tongue:
dead nettle, groundsel, mouse-ear,
ribwort, broadleaved dock,
decoded on my page, language
stipples mysteries of its own.

Fish that shiver pools in Spring:
lamprey, smelt, barbel, Allis shad,
are netted snugly in my threads
without the forfeiture of Come and Go.

Swinging moods that take their radii
from pendent heart are held:
love, happiness, betrayal, anguish, grief,
I claim them
with their names, mistress of their strength.

Yet set like gems in line and form:
sonnet, cinquain, englyn, villanelle,
words strike magic that I cannot hold,
give aura to the named, infinitely
heatseeking what is beyond the word.

Ding-Dong Bell

No rain this August. Dust rises underfoot.
In the hard earth cracks appear. There's talk
of rationing, remembered drought. The dead
walk close on the heels of memory.

At Poulaphouca drowned buildings lift.
Like longterm prisoners scan for sign,
case re-opening, new appeal, even the naming
of their unnamed crime. Sky is merciless,

holds them in the world's eye. Fraught
souls haunted by redemption, pleas,
like yours, exhuming guilt. After I killed you
I told it all in a book I buried

deep as ever well was dug. I wrote you off
far more ways than one, never gave thought
till now to the space where you lay hidden,
when August wakeful, in that back bedroom

iron bed, cross upon the wall, I sat up
again wrote in my ledger, can see it now,
'I told Teacher what you did today. She says
you're a bad girl. We've seen the last of you.'

Why couldn't you stay down there? Dead.

Ever Such

We had the bed bought
when she told us
its owners divorced,
'Ever such a sad story, though
it's good,' she said,

'as new, not a mark on it,'
we sought
evidence of discord
in its pale plump mattress,
the base

uncoupled
for ease of passage
up the turn on a staircase
round the angle
of a landing.

SIMMONS on the label,
the world's largest
makers of better
sleep products,
we doubted

testy springs
buttoned up
as secrets, eavesdropped
on their ghostly wranglings
as we turned over

after love,
your side only
stiff with a backboard,
mine sagging at the edge
where I sit to daydream,

every week
turn fresh sheets,
tweak to a crisp angle
a skirt of valance
know

on this lumpish mass
of hair and stitchery
we must make
shift
be glad on it.

Pickpocket
R. D. S. Spring Show

I could draw the face of loss
with a watercolour brush –

sable, hog's hair, squirrel –
and a wash of amber gold,

saving in one sweep
the face that swims to mind,

eyes the colour of whiskey,
a rash of freckles, the chin

vanishing, in my peripheral
a vision already in flux,

as I order strawberry milkshakes
at the Jersey Stall, feel for cash

in my gaping bag, the thief
a flashing salamander in the dust.

Sojourner

Everything is foreign at first

Even the light

Mouths make noises at me
It takes time to learn body language

A day tripper who has missed a connection
I carry the tags of a stranger

A family of Italians see my plight
'Io Paolo,' he says. I am embraced.
Adela pulls my sleeve, points to the cafe
We sip wine at a table in the sunshine
Their little boy eats ice cream
His fingers are sticky in mine

We give names to all the noises
I wear her shawl against the sudden chill

When my name is called on the intercom
I turn for home
With a heavy heart
Leave the shawl on a chair for her to find

Dust lifts in little circles on the runway.

Grey Area

For me there is no joy
discovering light can lie
skew-ways in the front room
of the interior
I took such trouble building.

Module by module,
openheartedly always
in full sun,
letting light in unimpeded
as a Holy Ghost.

What foolishness then
made me succumb
to the tattle of a sun-blind salesman,
'Accustom yourself to the dark,' he said,
'Think about the mushrooms.'

In gloom that first morning
after the light was sliced,
the candour of my bright room
dimmed, glory
holed up like dust in corners.

I grow accustomed now,
half-seeing, being half-seen,
I think about mushrooms often,
Mahon's mushrooms in a Wexford shed,
lungeing towards light.

While I squat and thicken,
up to my knees in grime,
follow the line of light
laterally, my skull
panned to a flat cap.

Butter Balls
for a sick child

On your bedside table sentinels,
Ampiclox, thermometer, syrup,
hourly change places. The rota

shakes down my fear,
                      steadies,
in the longest night, this watcher,
till stutter of your cough disrupts
for me the hush, breaks the casing

of a capsule.
                In the slow action, down
three flights of years, she lifts
muslin from the butter pat. Pieces
rolled in sugar on scrubbed deal

in her sweetened palm
                      are restoration.
Those remedies through parched lips
creaming the throat, ease my cough,
let me, and the household, sleep.

Mindful,
        she stirs the embers,
from an upright chair watches
for the future to whiten panes,
light quickening
                    her sleeping dynasty.

Heart Machine

The trick is to fix an eye
upward, let the mind desert
body, comically barefronted
in blue J-cloth, control box
taped around my waist, jellied
discs cold comfort on colder
fear, as end of tether heart
sorties on unmarked Parnassus.

Normal walking pace, she said,
left right left right forward feet
relax those shoulders, don't hold
the rail so tightly, up, up,
eyes stare at the picture,
La Route by Maurice Vlaminck,
leap from this trudging treadmill
into its onward stillness.

That roadway going nowhere
particular, so it seems,
between two cottage dwellings
and a covert of tall trees,
some surface gruesome blotching,
rust, or blood, residuals
of the fallen, but comfort,
no bodies by its borders.

Remember counting badgers,
dead badgers on the shoulder
of road to Ballinasloe,
one still trembled; that still body
on the tarmac at Dubai
till before the watching world
a plastic sheet made ghastly
carrion for steel-eyed bird.

May the road rise, ar dheis Dé,
only one in twelve gradient,
she said, but Vlaminck's roadway
leapt and snaked in the earthquake
of my breath, some robot hand
registering each seismic gasp
as foolish picot pattern
on a paper roll, don't slow,

slow, another thirty seconds,
you can manage can't you dear,
fearful bird in blinded flight
banged wildly on my chest wall
till I panted on the bed,
wondered what sprinkler system
operated from beyond
perforated firmament.

Face up, waited for its grace.

In Djouce Woods

Downhill from Calary Car Park –
a track so slippy
we held closely
toeholding among roots
brooding in slime
like tendencies.

These bifocal lenses
separating this descent
from common journeyings,
trees wore mourning too, bloodied
ruffs of fern, crepey frills.

Hillside paths wound down – terminal
zigzag stagger – through cloning pines
alike as sickbed days, always
the falling
waters. In the vee

we rested, rinsed resin from our fingers, lingered

Our ascent
so late we missed the children,
feared loss in muffling fog, sudden
as death, a brushoff
from boughs, sting of New Year's frost,
withheld tears.

Heaven to see light above,
step into a zodiac of headlamps,
children in the glow of campfire,
Joe, welcome and Lucozade,
to wipe the blur from lenses
find this darkness real.

Woman Seated Under the Willows
after a painting by Claude Monet

I'm afraid for you, woman.
He shows you the light

falls, goes on falling
always. On the move

in ribbons through willows,
pure blue in gloom

is a luminous fountain. Yellow
stipple from grass tips

beams up to slip along leaves
mizzles in droplets about you

and you wear a hat.

He touched you with red
to remind you of blood

and heat. Look, the same red
on that household you keep

in your middle distance.
What do you do? You

bury your head in a book.
I'm afraid for you, Woman.

Afraid for me.

Saturday Rugger Practice
Willow Park, Blackrock

The gulls are dispossessed,
take to the hills,
rally like White Boys for the hour

when blue and white hooped hordes,
who mimic battle on the sward, cease fire,
clamber bootless into waiting cars,

boast of places on the A's, the B's.
One pleads, 'Sure I wasn't useless
today, was I Daddy, sure I wasn't?'

when his father's mirrored eyes,
above the Puma tracksuit, new Rom runners,
relegate him always out of touch,

always on the sideline. I see him
too long tying his bootlace, whiling away
the mudstained hour, happy to leave it

all to the glory boys,
his gum shield sleeving rictus from the scornful,
his eyes on conkers in the long grass,

sunlight through sally leaves,
the last of swallows,
across the road the DART train south,

swift as opportunity, linear as life.
I want to shout when the ball comes
flying from a ruck, a heedless mill,

'Hold onto it, run with it,' duck
to sanctuary of birds, a try line
always further than you think, posts

like Pigeon House indicating upwards,
invite conversion through needle eye.
But, not often, everything comes together,

the ball's passed out along the line,
I find sureness, reason in it all,
poetry,

then studs, soundless on the turf's soft skin,
clatter onto tarmac, leave open wounds
where worms' turns pass unnoticed,

seed stirs uneasily, stretches to the light,
and cocksure gulls
with greedy eyes bide their time.

Basement

I

Even the footbeat its tempo slows
down the uncovered stair
where, in the deep heart's smallest hour,
shafts of memory colour a faded past,
through area panes white with paper lace,

here and there a square of red
cardinalises the tile of quarry floor,
burnishes the brass of taps, candlestick, switch,
yet hides from us the slime
of area walls, railed sky, glows

the Hotspur, drawbridge down, for toast
chuckling under portcullis seal, when home-
work done, I was Queen of the castle, walls
sweating peace and dream, till gravel rained
from that angular sky
as his car juddered home.

II

Jangle with broomhandle in wild declaration
the listless panel of dependent bells, labelled
Drawing Room, Nursery Floor, or Street Door,
hating now their silence then, and how he
used to thump upon the floor. Summon that

kitchen, maid's room off, where we danced,
Prosperity Song on the gramophone, the closet
where they said she'd slept, but when I dared,
fungus on the wall, toadstools big as cauliflowers,
the smell of pond weed. Oddments on a dresser,

a squint-eyed mirror for prink and frizz,
wiry hairbrush, home-perm rollers, spilled Tokalon,
Woolworth lipsticks in a biscuit tin, back of the hall
the room we called the Boot House, till peers eyeing us
askance at school, I buried it too (along with the gar-aj).

III

Pulp, blanch, sliver, crush, beat, chop,
a brewing from violence of verb only,
the pudding, its advent candied Christmas
in a glister of wishes, donkey-brown, till
sliced and fried with rashers from the ham.

My part the blanching, the plosive plopping
from the wrinkled skins, blamed all stolen
sweetness for the bitterness of almond after,
cherries, raisins, candied peel, only the suet
skinned for shredding was safe, till she

poured in porter, it smelled of him, and we
lost interest, left her to boil up
Christmas in a pillow sack, the cauldron
plumped and pluttered one whole day
flat irons on its lid, the walls beery.

IV

Raucously settling like roosting crows,
bare-legged gypsies homed, baking smells
the lure, from wayfaring summerdays long-
lasting as blackjack, crowded the sill, bars
that held the world in, stays

loosened at the top, through the dropped
fanlight of laced pane, she fobbed us off with
jam tarts, buying a safe hour for apple
pies to cool, bread to steam in a napkin
on the backyard sill, inside, under

its cross, the secret trace of treacle made
her bread our miracle, milk-
fed sucklings on the nethers of that basement, we
clawed at joy, were scalded
by her tongue, like hot jam.

V

Find me there, chthonic, knees under chin,
thumb in mouth, having recourse
where morning found trace of snail on
draining board, snails we raced on the back step,
tapping retraction on shells, as now past

voices beat on the membrane-stretch, their
muffled sticks unrhythmical, horning in,
upending the slimy netherworld for a new

careenage, caulking the gape of seams,
the way the breadman

left two pans between the railings (and she'd
eat the face off us for eating the heels
off them), with oakum picked from the old
ropes, umbilical, swaddling and apron strings
too twisted to be true, binding to be false.

Woman and Haystack
after a painting by Marc Chagall

The fireball sun flames my harvest
with licking tongues, lays claim to it,
but do I care?

Languid in a safe triangle
of sun and sickle and a daub of sky
I turn my back on it
rest assured

the fire I carry in my head
and in my belly yet
will more than challenge anything
it can throw at me, so

let it take my flagrant thighs
leave its mark on them

the haloing coolness of that long white arm
holds me in check

when I'm ready, in my own good time,
I'll match fire with fire.

A Cliché Called Death
– *Clogher Head, May 1993*

Some things have been thrown up
onto the long strand of today's poem.

They might have been symbols,
unique metaphors for themselves.

Razorbills, puffins, fulmars,
kittiwakes, Manx shearwaters,

dipped above their perfect images,
staying just long enough for me

to pick out in my seabird book,
name them. Familiars at Clogher,

they had the trustingness of their kind,
diving into their own element

the way I had their images dive
in mine. Their right? To be

transformed, preened to poetry
as at the dawn of original vision.

Their fate? Shrouding. In noxious oil
anonymous, line after line after line.

The Road to Navan

The road ahead peters. Illusion
rising in a vapour from the hedges

surrounds with fog the fields of vision.
Headlights are the Goldmann stars

with ever shorter tracks. Even
my good eye, narrowing, blurs,

sees purpose meld in speculation.
A truck passes, six-wheeler deluge

on my windscreen. Water. This again.
Breaking waters and an engine thrum,

bearing me, blind, in some propulsion.
Mind moves all things sweetly. Joy is

light's stable halo at Dunshaughlin
and the dark ray of road beyond.

Non-Verbal Arts
– Derry, 1993

On Derry City's wall, the camera
pins me to Verbal Arts, studiously
ignores graves in St. Columb's shadow.
Runic oak trees flex their roots

as far south as Cork City, a schoolgirl
rooted to an oak desk weeps
for the Siege of Derry, its citizens,
the soldiers, A Child's History Of Ireland,

dips her Waverley nib in the well,
draws crosses, crosses, crosses,
a wall of crosses, a Foyle of crosses,
rivering the page to wordlessness.

At the Orchard Gallery – Derry
for Brian Kennedy

Broken glass embedded in concrete
Designed to repel apple scrumpers?

Fjords of glass, phallic, invasive
As longboats to lush interiors.

Giant splinters' mega capacities
Transvest an army of Snow-Queens.

Gritty crystals, treacherous as ice,
Scandalise the carpets.

You tell me how we can traverse
This sharp forest unknifed. Who

Passed this way before us
Like a wand. Laying on of hands

Remembered in the slant of light,
As filigree of love or chrism. Grace.

Miss Tynan to Willie Yeats

On those nights, your father, weary,
(the light turned taupe over Harold's Cross),
called on you to clean his brushes,
'Not linseed, numbskull! Turpentine!'
bade me stay. In a narrow cot

my body, thawing from the studio pose,
appalled with languor, clutched
at rigid Guardians. Maybe I dreamed
you, *night-dark* and *eager-eyed*,
all *dreams and gentleness*, passing me by

on the road, stress and unstress of your lope
controlling distance, I followed, meekly,
a feminine ending. *My Dear Katey*
vainly matched her heartfelt measures
to *Dear Miss Tynan*, years too soon.

Waking from this dream of spondees,
their rise and fall pounded in ears
like heart-blood. Fear drained slowly
when I heard through the thin wall, you
chanting to yourself, monotonously,

in the dark watches, each soul cries out
its mentor. Praise or supplication.
Pater Noster on my lips, you call on Milton,
Of Man's first disobedience and the fruit ...
Is it your father mutters, 'Light! Light!'?